SALOME

AND THE

BATTLE

POEMS

TYLER ROSE MANN

Salome and the Battle Poems

Published by Bayonet Press, New York

First Printing, 2018

ISBN 978-0-692-11122-2

Cover design by Tyler Rose Mann and Võ Minh Quân

For *MR*, *always*.
For *WP*, who showed me it was possible.
For *HH*, for the infinity of gifts.

"For the lips of an immoral woman
are as sweet as honey,
and her mouth is smoother than oil.
But in the end she is as bitter as poison,
as dangerous as a double-edged sword."

Proverbs 5:3-4

Table of Contents

VENGEANCE

Backwriting the Map

If you listen I'll tell you everything:

How the Skirt Girls stood with their hands on their hips,
casting stones at the outcasts
with our hands in our laps and inside each others seams
and up under everything
that could change the morning's flavor.

I will tell you I found the Lord
between her legs, everything that had run from me
afloat there. I called her Savior
but if they start after you with a loaded gun,
you better run before they get all the rounds in.

She didn't even go after the first clip.

She called me Firefly, cuz she confused
the firefight with fireworks.

> *Firefly*
> is how I signed her ransom notes.

She wrote me love letters.
She pressed them to my throat like they were potions.
She thought she might believe in God. She quoted psalms
to herd me from my head.
I kept her close
so she could watch me rotting in her palms.

If you want me to I'll tell you about the Junkyard Boys,
running rabid on their chains
letting lose their savage stomachs,
pumping petrol in their veins,
thinking circle wild's the same as skyline free.

I'll testify about these ugly things,
how we held them to the light hoping to find
the fault lines and the breaker switches,
and now we are onebyone toppling,
our domino bodies landing flat
or tumbling too far gone.

I will tell you that I was born like this:
the cracks that itch in my skull begging for spells
& how we stoppered up our hurt in bottles
& some of us washed out to sea.
Now I'm left dry at the shoreline
wondering if someone will find the broken bodies
and tell me what the message was, those five years
of fists and firebellies
that I still cannot bring myself to write about.

But if you want to hear it I will speak
about the monster in my mind,
how I tried to keep it quiet with the whiskey & the boys,
          all these flammable excuses.
I can show you the scars that stepladder up my arms,
how each one is a padlock on a door my mother prays
that I will never open.
I'll show you the hinges, how they swing
          ecstasy, agony
and I swear every time that the highs are worth the ride
until I am plummeting towards that purple portal,
I am clawing at the doorframe,
          sorry mama
          but I will take the permanence
          if I can give away this burden on my back.

There are days
when the blood in my veins feels like theft
and I have not earned my stay inside my skin yet,

scuffing through unlikely love that I do not deserve.

If you listen you can hear the thunder through the thorns,
hear the soft spaces churning into something
hard to snap.
I am trying to stitch it all into something sensible to wear
& pricking my fingers on the spiteful pieces.

I am not sure if you are thinking of me as
cliffside, unclimbable
or more like a raft, thrashing
in black waters but I am more like a firespinner:
there is rhythm
and pattern
and a path that I followed
and now I am backwriting the map
and if you ask me to,
I will tell you everything.

Pool

My mouth is a cue ball.
My teeth are coral reefs
that my words break against, when
the tides of my speech
follow the moon.

(I rage in tidal waves,
love in currents.)

I used to prop my cheekbones up
with compliments, stuff
Cosmopolitan photo spreads
crumpled into my waistband
so now when I dance to thunderclaps,
I see airbrushed dreams
dribble down my thighs
to stain the parts of me where
there are no marks
          yet.

My mouth is a cue ball, because
I didn't do so well as an 8-ball
and when we pass as strangers in the street
I am wondering if we would make good lovers
& if your hands would know how to touch my scars
& how would you stand up to the strike?
          Are you a bumper?
          Or a cue stick?

I tell you my mouth is a cue ball
Because I saw him turn her face into a battlefield
& a blue swell
& I am through with bruised.
So these days you only catch me in straight lines
on diagonal destinations.

They tell me gravity
is one hell of a drug.
      Well.
      This is an object in motion.

So now I'll play the boys like billiards.
I am finished getting knocked around.

Touch

I don't want you to touch me.

      Except when I do.

Except when my skin needs a salve
for the silence.

But I don't want you to know about the bruises,
how my bones all bent backwards.
I don't want you to see all the holes in the walls
and then call yourself spackle
or plaster.

When I say you cannot hurt me, I am not bragging.
I am describing the architecture,
how the windowpanes were all broken out
and I was left with the just the frames and this
      brick house.

I am saying the edges are all sharp now
and there are 2 people in this world
who were able to fit their feet between the breakage,
who made footholds out of missing pieces,
and I broke them both.
I don't want you to know how they begged me to stay,
how I walked away from their bodies like blast craters
because my body is a bomb,
every inch of its machinery ticking towards casualty
& the last time that
he touched me wrong
and I don't know how to tell you
where to put your hands instead.

The last man who saw me naked

did not even ask where the scars came from.
He was a soldier
so I thought he was a warrior
but he was a coward
afraid to be honest unless it was base
and I had to explain that under dim light
or a dirty room
the naked truth can still be beautiful
and I don't need to hear about your mother
for you to touch me like you had one,
like some grown woman skinned her knees
over the making of you into a man.

He did not understand.

I need you to understand
that your hands can brush over my canvas only
if you can imagine the colors.
I do not want you to see the chaos
unless you call it collage.
I am waiting for someone to see the jagged edges
and tumble me into seaglass.

No, I am not asking for permanence
or for you to hang me in your living room.
I want you to take off my porcupine suit and
beg me to scream my poetry out loud
because you know that this stage
is the only place that you have ever truly seen me naked
and that I don't want you to touch me

except when I do.

The Edge of the Knife

On the day that you swallowed me
it is true that I collaborated with your teeth,
leaned against your molars
hoping you would see my meat
and call it feast.
I had hoped to make a soft spot of a fiend,
hoped you would unwrap me and savor my nature,
gnaw on my bone structure,
but knew no other way to be beautiful
than to tie myself to bedframes
and call it ballgown.

But when my kindling limbs were splitting into splinters
you called them toothpicks
and let the stack ignite.

I did not want to be devoured.
I did not want to smokestack for cloud cover,
did not want to have to pray for rain to satiate the blaze.
You called me firewood
and I knew no better way towards warm than up in flames.
You called me lover
while I chewed away my arms
to flee the crushing boulder I lay under.
I called my mother
but you pressed me under all your ugly weather
and locked me in your closet
with all your other crumpled laundry
and now I am discovering
ten years of termites
have been eating away
at all the safe places in my body
and I used to see your face on the edge of all my blades
and knew that I had to cut you out

before you devoured me.

Now I am so tired of keeping you with me.
I am so sick of how you've been sleeping under my skin
and bruising all my freckles into bulletholes.
I am so tired of wishing you
into something weeping and kneeling,
how my knives would find
the soft places behind your eyes
and carve them into something sinister:
> a simple slice for every night I cried
> over things you snatched
> that I had to build back from scratch over
> ten years
> crawling

out of that powerless pit in the ground
where the water all flowed

so when my sob stories became too waterlogged
to hold onto without drowning
I turned them into sailboats.
And on the dark days
my flag still keeps a skull with crossbones
and we are are a warship
slipping scalpel-slick through dark night
> but I will emerge upright
> > and dripping with daylight
> > and dancing

> and now my orgasms are orchestras!
every symphony begging me
to write treaties to my own bones
so I am kissing the places where the joints rub,
forgiving the stubbed toes for the blunt ache,
transforming the sharp shame
into something I can scrape clean enough to sleep on.

And I have considered
how it would feel to have healing plunge
into my hurt depths
but I am not ready yet
to be left with nothing but smoothness and round
when I am nursing a new rage in my belly
that is not afraid of its own name or a new slice
and why would you be something for me to "survive"
when you were made to cower in corners
and I am the edge of the knife?

Salome

They called me harlot.

They saw my hips switch,
silk scarves swinging into battle axes
sharp enough to cut through kings ambition,
how my breasts swelled with power
the bought queens never dreamed of.
They saw the veils drop,
each one a knife wound in a beer gut.

They called it slut.

First they tied my mother to the whipping post and tried her
for her heartstrings stretching to a second marriage,
womb already wasted on a daughter.
My mother keeps a high chin
strutting down cobblestones that spit back the slurs,
how the men on the corners
tugged the romance from her braids
and stuffed it into sinful.
My fingers curl into the fist she keeps tucked in her stomach,
all those stones she's swallowed.
My kept mother weeps through her dreams
while her king bargains for babbling women
to discard by daylight,
so I dance til my own dawn,
peeling off layers til I am left with nothing but bone marrow
luminous with moonlight and mischief.

The sixteen years that kissed my frame have settled
in soft places that men stare at
like my skin wasn't just a pillowcase or picture frame,
my mind a meek afterthought like the wives
who mew like mice and nibble at the gossip trickles,

my mother's lover the nougat
so they had to suck her dry to stopper up their sour.

I never asked to be sugar water,
but I won't let them drink my mother down.

And when I dance the women stand around and pout
like they can't see me beating out and drumming up
        a battlefield
and they could stand on my side if they pleased.

You know the Baptist caught coins for his sermons
and I have spied him preying on the so-called "sinful ladies"
like we don't sit in cages waiting to be hand-plucked
before we wither. I'll be the stalk of thorns
that you can twist around the crowns of kings.
        Call it sin.
           Call it slut.
                I'll take the head and call it even.
You can follow the blood splatter to the barracks
where I will squat with my teeth bared
and wait for dusk to muster up its courage and ask me
sheepish
if I'll dance for them again.

They say that blood stains its beggars,
the burgundy bruise a bright line on a scoreboard
with the Lord for a keeper.
Well.
You tell Him that I carry my shames
in a sack that I swing from my waist
and all the weight helps me gyrate,
all my guilty gravity balancing my mother's scales.
You tell Him I write down righteousness on my own slate
and so long as I am keeping score,
I will make the morals match their messengers

and use my hated form to fit a freer function.

I tell you I never asked to be a gift horse
but here we are.
And if I can wield shields out of silk scarves
and tap treaties out of temptation,
I will shimmy out of
every set
of seven veils
and call myself the queen.

They called me harlot, the bible bending away
from my true name to keep me naked in the photographs
but I am a wildfire and not an open wound.
I was meant to burn and not be covered.

Ask for the woman whose ballet shoes
        turned a battalion into ashes.
Ask for the woman with the knife knees,
        with the bullets for a backbone.
I sift souls through my hair like a silver comb,
        and for this they called me whore.
        But my name is Salome.

Ghost

So he's turned you into a rolling joke
a picture frame alone and unsold on an empty wall
and waiting for a Midas call to transmute to gold
the muleish hoofback and kickup
of sticking your neck out
over a canyon of pride
and the lonesome solitude that clings to the roots
of your hair when you rinse.
You have been scrubbing away at the stain
of your Sisyphus aching up love's cliffsides
and renting out your skin
for the price of a night's bridge
& placing your stories up on impatient pedestals,
wishing him to unveil you & inquire
about your earthliest origins.

So he's turned you into an abandoned astronaut
with all the world as your womb
but crying instead for the quick caress of a man
who has never carried your water
quivering through his eager fingers
& also never truly twisted your spine
into climbing bubbles of ecstasy and ease,
never witnessed your magic as a free woman
twisting the world in her fist
to wring bliss out of hopelessness & hard hustle
& remembering
          somewhat
          still
to try & unwind & unclench your gamble hands
to let the holdings float
and air out the bad habits
that cling still
          always

every dawn deep
to your wide & shapeshift skin
with its fruit bruises
that burst even under the pressure of pleasure.

So he turned your desire against a grindstone
and pressed you into a pillar
but he has none of the boldness of a sculptor
or an honest artist sticking by their mistakes
and sealing all the firm letters with sincerity's hot wax.
He is hiding behind invisible glass,
those fragile walls dividing his `
mural mansion facade into prison cells
and your hurricane rain would have
washed away the paint and flooded
his shallow storm drain
so there's no sense in swimming through the confusion
to break into rooms that always would have been
too coward crush
for the bounty of your brave breath.

So he's turned your singing hours into a foolish acapella
as though you were howling at his moon
and not snapping at his temporary metronome,
like his tired pop song turned you into a river dancer
when you were just wading through his pond water
to get to the roaring ocean

so you don't be keeping your time
with his timid tides
when alone,
your own rhythm
     flows
         so
            steady.

TENDERNESS

Queen Alyssa-Rea

My niece hovers between light and heat,
her mothers staving off the void,
holding up the trapeze with their wingtips
so the balancing act
will only ever look like a magic trick.

My niece swings at the strings of adolescence
while her mothers grasp at the straws of blessings
to bestow them as the hand me downs they never had.

My niece comes from a line of backbone women
free-fall women who catch cliffsides
with the force of their fingers.
Her mother erects metal monuments
that are sealed in concrete.
I walk up the steps of the buildings she creates,
see the sharp of her hips in the corner creases,
the hard floorboard of her mouth on a workday,
vanishing point of her smile lines on a due date

My niece climbs the iron girders of her mother's ribcage
to see the sunrise.

My grandmother chiseled meaning from marble.
while sickness sucked at the marrows of her bones.
She chipped stone into statues
that still stand in her absence,
and now my niece paints pictures of rainbows
with their legs on dissimilar shores.
She goes wherever her aunt goes,
        or so she tells me.
She sends me her landscapes by post,
I trace her paint strokes
and wonder which side she'll land on.

Her horizon expands
every minute her mother spends away at war
and she stands in the hallway
measuring the distance between them on the map,
tap-tapping her small feet and feeling the time stretch
into dental floss, into doctors notes,
milestones and missing teeth.

My niece is a rainshower
and her mother feels the ghost of drops on her skin,
squatting battle-ready in summer sun,
her wife sweating through American labor,
blister-blue on harness lines
so my niece can have something to hang on to.

My niece paints her nails the color of oceans
because she comes from a line of women
who have sailed across seas to seek salvation,
built bridges with the span of their spines.
We drum doorways out of dead dreams,
crush courage into our cuticles.

My niece was born with a shield on her back.
Her mothers spoon-feed her swords every morning.
They keep a calendar of days since her birth,
every tally is a tiger stripe.
My niece is worth that weight in starlight,
in serendipity and second chances.
Her matriarchs are made of mountains,
foreheads frosted with snowfall,
feet planted firm.

My niece was born in a battlefield.
Her body built up in a blast crater.
Her body collateral for capitalism.
Her mothers' bodies are bishops, clearing the game board

so she can move in all directions.

My niece is no chess piece.

My niece comes from women
who chip their teeth on concrete and spit out pearls.
My niece has eyes like the world, grass green
because she will learn to fight like a woman
and go where she please like a queen.

Rosetta Stone

I know all the poetry of bread and cigarettes
and addicts with their empty eyes
and I can spot them all the way across a bar or bridge.

This boy, his throat be a birdsong.
His freedom is a fishing line.
My hands are full of gifts
and there are not enough collarbones or crescent moons
to give to.

I want to collapse his synapses into a constellation song
that snaps like the galactic guitar.
I dreamed of the ways that we would press our time
into paintstrokes and eighth notes,
how my stomach has been waiting
for someone to see its sheet music
and play me from sarcophagus to symphony.

I am not sure if he is really starlight
or just silhouette and shadow puppet,
the man on the moon that my mind is making up
out of two potholes and a clothesline connection
because I am ready to string bedsheets up on anything
that looks like it's come from my block
and brought the baggage too, that blessed suitcase
stuffed with all the savage scrolls
I cannot bear to burn because they are Rosetta stone
and my heart is written in hieroglyphs
that I am sick of spelling out into rooms
full of eyebrows and open mouths, but I swear
I am much more meadow than citadel
if you can speak the language
that any of my stories are written in.

Ask me what I see in him.
I will ask if you can speak with your neighbors.
I will ask if you, too, live in a room
in a building
        in a city
                in a state
                        in a whole marching nation
where no one knows your name
but they can all tell you've got an accent.
I will ask if your skin, too, is tattooed with trackmarks
that you call free weights
        or "freckles"
depending on who is listening.

I will ask you who is listening.
Whether they, too, have traumas
they have trained their tongues around
because they don't fit in the caves
of anyone else's experience.
I will tell you that we were refugees
from the same slaughterhouse
and I don't know anyone else whose eardrums
rattled with the bomb sounds.
I will tell you that I had tucked a tumor full of truths
down my trachea
and he was the needlepoint that burst me into a bard,
bubbling over with all of the bile
that I have been biting back for so many years.

I'll tell you that his tongue circled
over all those cutting consonants
and moaning vowels
that I have not pronounced in so many alphabet rounds
when so many speakers of my mother tongue are martyrs
and I don't want to know another ghost.

Too many of the men I used to know,
either still swimming in the whiskey fishbowl or else
pulling their hearts out from the back ends of syringes
and I was handed this new life as a glass gift.

So *of course*
I will kiss your forehead and call the mark a crown!
there is not enough time
for the merry-go-round of save-face and masquerade
when my blood whistles like a cross country train!
My love beat like rain on tin roofs
& the sound is the loudest embrace you ever slept under,
        boy, *I swear*
        my arms are *open*
for all your comings and your goings
if you just call me by my name,
facing forwards.

Love in Rainy Season

By December the rainy season had dried out into a drizzle. The monsoon storms with all their beastly screeching and flooding had spread themselves out thin, how the trapped and starving spare their rations to drag the stomachache out to a tapered end.

Jack London said he would rather burn out in an instant than gather dust over an eternity. Still, stranded, even the hedonists would moderate. But not everything can go. "Exhaustible supplies" are sparingly consumed. Spirit keeps on pouring in, waterfall on infinite.

Yet here we are, champions of smalltalk.

The rain patters absentmindedly out our open window today and yesterday and tomorrow, tapping a background to our mindless chatter. We haven't slept together in months. You've put on weight and I've put on an attitude. Invisible drops in a hateful barrel. But the streets don't flood anymore.

I dream relentlessly of another man.
Every morning I feel less like a thief.

I've never been on a love that didn't capsize. I'm one to sink the ship, swiss-cheese it with lead-holes after I've mutinied and stolen the lifeboats. Every lover swimming in my wake calls me a pirate. Scream like thunder, sob like a storm.

But not you.

The country is driving and biding its time under cheap plastic ponchos. Every goddamn thing in this city is damp. Our belongings are growing mold, turning gray and ill-defined, takeover on timelapse.

When I told you I had to leave, you didn't even blink. You only asked me to keep the peace. I gaped at you, like at a politician.

Even I keep my favorite fruits until they rot, save the last hot sips til they've gone cold. You always thought that was neurotic. To love something so much you wait until it's no longer itself. You always gulped the last dregs down, salvaging my wasteful scraps.

Yet here we are, dissolving into mist.

The monsoon storms with all their flooding and loving
have spread themselves out thin.
Everyone is waiting.
Our quiet country, just waiting for the rains to stop.

Love is Not Enough

Whoever said that life is too short to have regrets
must have only lived one time
because on this, the last of my nine lives,
the wreckage is piled so high behind me
I don't even bother with the rear views

But I don't have to look back to see you
when your ghosts float before me every day.
We have both taken to Twitter to take down our halves
of conversations that no longer have a place to stay.
I watch you this way: the paintings on the walls
of your skull that used to be full of my portrait.
There is no telling what you have kept,
whether there is a room for me that is neat and well-swept
or unkempt and curtained. I analyze
the secondhand snippets of you that I receive
until they no longer look like themselves.
Every day I grow more into a self I know that you would like
because it could love us both better.

You used to tell me you liked the color
of your hands on my thighs
and I wonder if now you marvel at another lover's color too
but this time because she brings out the light in you
and you are learning that darkness never even suited you
unless it is what you carry on your own skin
and that True Love is not a synonym
for compensating for someone else's sins.

          "But I was made for this!"
you told me once,
piecing us both back together on your own.
And maybe that was so,
but that was long ago before you yet believed

that you deserved more than I could give.

I have always told you this:

Your fingers were meant to fold over a future
full of easy blessings. Instead,
when you stayed steadfast I was second-guessing,
reaching out our open windows,
heart unsteady.

I am not regretting the leaving of it,
only the times we drove each other into ditches,
twisting in the angry hedges,
weeping when we could be drinking in
the laughter of the day.
I am not regretting walking away, saying
         love is not enough.
I am regretting your echo shouting back
at the wall of my back:
         "but it could be!"

Only one of us would give it all for love and it was never me.

By the time I stumbled through your open doorway
I was already dissolving into a baseball game,
         always going, never gone.
You crucified yourself into open arms until you moved on
the last time I made you let me go.

This is my prodigal summer, the sun
spying on our separation.
There are no second chances to stake out.
I walked out from our house and into the mouth
of a life that might be a mistake,
and might save me.

You are not a part of this equation
but I cannot subtract you at the source.
I am pulling your threads out from my seams;
          you are sewn into *everything*.

Love was not enough to make me stay
but it is the lining on the soles of my feet.

I have set myself free.
I am taking you with me.

Goodbye

The five finger flag at the end of my arm
is waving you onwards
even while my bones fold forwards
for another one of your blessings,
how my heart was a sunflower
yearning into your yellow
and forgetting to grow towards the riot
of my own loud light.

Now I am alone in this washboard city
where all the wounds get rinsed out and redressed
but there's something toothless in the embrace
and no one to gnaw over the loss with,
wondering anyway if you would find me foolish
for always searching for the sandpaper
under the shine.

You will get my grit out from under your nails.
You will cough up the wishbones that caught in your throat,
dry the flooding of the panic basement,
keep the waterstains on all the photographs,
the crisis with the kisses.

I am wishing feathers onto my replacement's arms,
praying you pin me up to a corkboard
with your bad test scores and move past our college try
to find the conjugal kindness you've built a nest for.

I am sure I'll heave the sorrow along with my debt
til me or the bank is bankrupt and bust.
But there is a woman here whose heart is a dandelion:
one quick breath might blow her away,
and the risk is worth the wishes.
There is a man whose hands

turned my tragedies into marbles
and while we rolled over and over the cool spheres
I was skipping the last of your stones out of my soul
into a lake I'll swim in again
but not today.

Today I am breaking my own heart
like peeling stuck paper apart
or a wet sticker from its wasted back
and I am aching like a freight train
wailing down roads the wheels don't want to go

and I am still grieving and keeping the trinkets
and stealing the solace from my own sick chest
every moon I have not quit you yet
but yesterday I left the door open to daylight
and it came inside.

The lonely ain't left me alone yet
but I am slipping out back to belong to myself again
leaving notes in the kitchen all wishing you
goodbye.

Elegy for JJ

After seven years I still wear your clothes
and your shorts still sag at my hips
because they too are missing something
to hold them up.

If only you could see us now!
Sails up to send our vessels East.
Some of us have gotten free
but you were a bonsai tree caught
in the wrong greenhouse.
In the drought all of our twisted trunks
tilted towards the same trap,
but we had wrapped the grass around our fingers.
We held tight. You sat tied
inside a terra cotta pot,
that collar you were born to.

Writing this poem I see your bloodlines in the ink,
how your mother smoked white & birthed you
                into a bottle.
She pulled you out in spurts and splatters,
stuffed you back inside.

You looked like your mother.
You and your mother looked for each other
in the bottoms of bags,
                altars of aluminum foil,
                        curled up over a mirror—
—when were you here with us?
Or were you oxidizing into rust
from the moment you met her?
every night you go back to the pipe like a smoke ribbon,
our ill-gotten genie bearing no gifts.
Already I am forgetting the length of your hair,

which snaggletooth snuck out of your smile.
I have no pictures of your face.
I feel it slipping away
down the back of my throat like a sour drip
I can't catch. I am afraid it will slide
into my stomach acid and burn away.
I am ashamed of the other memories
    I did not mean to keep:

Your head, blood buried in my lap
    in the backseat of a car
    driving from one downhill to the next,
Your body tossed against their trunk
    bruised and double-braceleted,
The broken beg of your voice
    scraping the dregs of your pride for
    "just one line,"
Your frustrated fingers
    forcing a bent needle into a tired vein—

    —none of us were the same after those years
but you were born different.
Your infant skin shook with the cravings, dopesick
before you had a name.

There is no coming back from this,
how the sun was always tar-colored,
how my glasses keep pink lenses
so the far bends always look like a rosebed,
how yours was always the deep end,
yours shivered under spider webs,
your deck was short cards and you were still counting,
cuz we all knew there would be no re-deal.

I panhandled a ticket out and took it.

I left you all split knuckled over scraps before the ax fell.
I left you gasping in the clutches of a maze
I knew you would not escape.
I left you auctioning your sky to buy your own kryptonite.

I left you.

& I still wake wheezing and blind from the dreams
where the machine guns sweep over everyone
and you all drop to your knees, crumpled into piles
of dirty clothes and slaughtered dreams
and I stand screaming in the center:
        so selfishly sorry,
        so wastefully spared.

I think you'd like it here.
Or maybe not.
Maybe we'd all look like marks to rob
and I can hear you telling me that I've gone soft,
but I think you'd love me even so.
Or maybe no love goes unbroken when the bridges burn.
Maybe riverbanks are boundaries, neatly kept.
Maybe you'd have never left
and we'd escape upstream, wondering
if it would be a bullet or a bad batch.

Maybe you could never love us now.
But I am remembering how the world was a shark's mouth
and I cut my feet on all its rows of razor teeth.
Your own hands were daggers, but I believe
you wished to keep your body
between the beast and me.

If only you could see us now, sails up
to send our vessels out anywhere they'll go!
Some of us have let our hair grow out,

some of us have settled down.
And I know that you'd still be a genie in a bottle.
I know that you aren't looking down from any cloudy tower.
I know that your clothes get more mileage
on my own moving frame
than any of the same traps your black hole body set,
that these days I should take what I can get
even if it's just me.
Even if I am alone watching Sodom burn,
watching the flames creep up from the base of your mast
wondering who I could have saved
if I just went back home
                              to the fire.

It's two years since you've been gone
and I hold on to the waistband of your pants
because I can hold them up myself.

Sails up.

If only you could see us.

PHOTOSYNTHESIS

One Face, Two Face

She told me that all bad people are just good people
on a strange path,
and all the saints are just secret keeping sinners,
or mediocre folks
who never woke up on the odd side of the road:
Exceptional Evil is only the bedfellow of
Ghandian Greatness.

I told her the saints had been such selfish lovers lately.
She said, *you've got two hands,
do it yourself.*

He told me that travel is stupid
because the only thing it can ever teach you is that
everyone is exactly the same
in different headwraps & ways of weaving floormats
& bathroom habits
but at the end of every day all everyone wants
is a hot meal a good fuck a stiff drink & a cuddle
to feed their pets & eat the rest
and get on with it.

They all want to tell me about their Stuff,
how they used to have so much
but now they just want to go fishing
and drink topshelf liquor at thirdworld prices.
They all just want to wear harem pants
and fill their pockets
with the little white seashells
that wash up on the beach in clusters.

We all want to tell about our bad habits,
how we tore them off like bandages and new skin
bloomed underneath them.

Scars are just new masks, I say,
but that is a very unpopular opinion.

When we sneak away into our seashell stashes
we rattle them in our hands
like underwater windchimes
and imagine how they sounded
clattering up and away from the ocean

Some days when I look at the ocean
she is a quilt of belonging
ivory infinity folding over and over itself.
Other days she is the silver specter of regret
and a thousand seashells thrown into her mirror face
get gobbled up
with only gagging bubbles
for protest.

Be the Joy

The yogi tells me I have earned it.
She tells me this pause, and this breath,
        I deserve it.
Through the sweat & the aches
of this class and this life
that this space is MINE
to cherish and MINE
when my hands are pressed at my chest
to make what I please in this pose that
for once
is no prayer,
        but release.

So I squeeze
together two tired palms—
        art-heavy, work-weary—
and I break
when she says:

"YOU
in this moment
glisten sweatbeautiful
in the wake of all the work
& every fateful mistake.
So let the love in."

She said:
        "let yourself love yourself"

so my grin cracks through
the tears and the strain and the breaks
in my back
to teach me that

        THE HURT IS WORTH IT.

That scar tissue
is really just a bridge
over a bleeding gap. &

IT IS ENOUGH   *

if I am the only one
out here who can see
the clawtunnels & the toothmarks
because I am carving & paving my way
in foxholes and gardens
to this life that I love because
            I wove it.
            clean and whole.
with two dirty & beautiful hands
from a brokenbottle rockbottom basement
from spite & spit & fists
when I turned slit wrists to sunrises.
when I buried my dead.
and I moved onwards.

            and upwards.

            towards daylight.

Now,
I want to overflow!
with health and gold
and make the life that I was told
      I'd never live to.

Now,
I want to bloom!
into the culmination of all the things
that I have ever loved
      or broken,
that I created or
      I killed.
caressed & coaxed or
      violent willed,
From every cell of my own skin
that my hands tried to destroy,
I'll bend and change to feel the joy!
Now, I want to *be* the joy!

Braille

This chest is cavernous.
Even undressed I look like the mess
I used to make of my life
and still might
if I don't play all my cards
       just right,
these red and white lines,
my crosshatched cartography of catastrophe
that I've covered myself with like a cloak of misfortune

I wear my wars.
I strap every wound I have ever won to my skin
like a badge of honor, a coat of armor
a scarlet letter.
My museum of missteps.
My collage of misplaced rage.
A map of every fidget my hands made
into some place I didn't intend

because I can think myself off a cliff or a blind bend
and wake up broke-boned in the sharp morning
wondering how it happened
       just the same as the last time
because these hands are motorboats
that I drag behind
on my unwieldy skis, tripping over the wake
& pulling all the collateral love down
behind me

At night I trace the lines in ink and think
of who possesses parallels.
My body the voodoo doll, always saying farewell
to another pricked person every time I stick myself.

I left him stitching up my riptide when I split,
cleaning after all my seismic shifts.

Nobody can live this way.

I don't know what happens when I run out of canvas space.

There is no hiding from this now.
I wear the fractal pattern fractures
on all the walls of my body's house.

I spit my secrets every night into this city's mouth,
        but you don't hear me.
I strip and show my soul off to the crowd,
        but you don't see me.

So undress me.
We can trace a road map with our fingertips
& you can kiss my histories.
That's how you read the poetry
that my body's pushing out in braille.

Letter to the Artist from the Muse

It isn't meant to be easy
the stringing of these beads of suffering
into something that hangs from your throat,
this noose, this necklace,
this crushing blessing, blazing burden on your back

      I will colonize your body.

Your mouth will be the welcome mat.
you have been assembled piecemeal from parts
to perform like a puppet
to parade the ugly things that sleep inside your bones
and it is true that you are one for square shoulders
that does not scare or stumble

      but I will strip you

and you will regurgitate your secrets,
tripping on the heaving cracks
pressing your camel's back against the weight
of past tenses

      The opening will feel like a gash
      even when it is a gateway.

My art will open your arteries.
You will bear the ache with grace.
Your heart will be a catalyzing acid
and the chemicals will sear on their way to electric.

When they give you sick pieces of themselves
that you've unearthed with my alchemy
you will hold them in your hands
like they were last-breath

because they are underwater and you
are painting them pictures of daylight,
their salvation tunnel carving itself out
of your awful aching depths.

You can let the terror well up tidal in your chest
and fill you up into an aching bowl of inaction
or pour your honest hot into the live pan.

This is the end of the road.

You can stifle in your own sick smoke or fall into the flames.
When you are roasting, I will toast you golden.

The Alchemist

It is 2018 and my bloodstream be bursting with bravery!
I look my failings in the face.
I walked away from a love that was the whole lining
of my heart lake
and I let all the water flood out
just so I could stop floating in it like a withered fish
and find the bottom stones to walk upon alone.

I am Moses.
I am splitting myself open to cross over the ocean
to search for other water on another side.

Now my lonely aches like a knife wound
but I would still rather collide with you and separate
than turn your holy weight into another ball and chain
Rather paint myself into an old maid
alone and seeking god in solitude and stars
than press your fingerprints too long into my skin.
I won't convert your stream into a home stretch
won't pave my road with temporary cobblestones
won't let my drops of larger longing build into a bucket
that I will call regret,

won't take these boots off.

I am kicking the door down.
With this skin that has been synonym
for so much that I wish I could take back
but I am unlearning the ugly things.
I am breaking my way into a new life
like a thief in the night sliding
all my bad habits out the back door.
I am a magician dissolving my sins into ozone
& eating them back up to spit out oxygen –

poetic photosynthesis.

I am so afraid that I am an ember burning away
at both ends & the hot days
will absolutely turn me to ashes.

But I am burning anyway

because my body was a battlefield
before breasts bloomed on my chest
to beckon the boys blind to their better manners.
My body is a warzone
& the boys wanna blow it to bits
if they cant kiss it & the spectators watch & hiss
at me tapping my own tin drum
to tell about the touches on the mountain
and tut tutting their tongue at my boot camp songs,
how nobody else sings along
until they break over the border into bruised, too.

But I stay singing.

& every morning
I strip the lonely
from my longing arms
and strap the warpaint on
my grieving, grinning face.

There is a man now who hears his hands in my poems
& now he's *so sorry* for how he used them
so sorry for tossing me flopping in the fishbowl
so sorry for pressing up against my peace
to lay his guilt out at my feet
& sway & suck his teeth
when I keep the grudge

Now my swords swim sharp through the ether.
I am a blacksmith
hammering hot words from hard iron
        and you will listen to them live,
hear my my barking bomb dogs tugging at your ear lobes
when you lay your head to rest.
I told him *no*,
        I am not finished
        with the poems yet.

But I will let the scabs seal over into art forms
that you can wrap your arms around.
I wish to be an anchor and a light house,
I want my darkness to splash out across the walls
        as shadow puppets
I stretch the gaps between my cells and gasp:
        Make me a conduit for all the awful things
        to right their sharpened surgeries to harmonies!

I will bear up under the weight
in my clay house made by hand
holding the whole sky on its back and
slanting horizon bound with the burden of starlight
and the impossible depth
of astronomical nothingness.

I live in the irreconcilable margins of two worlds:
too tooth and talon for the petal girls
& too tarnished by the silver polish of privilege
for black boys & boneyards.
All of my covetous greed, marching upwind and rainfaced
to translate these gifts into gospel,
chisel these improbable origins into a stone tablet
that you can call rowboat or broadsword
because I am both prophet and banshee,
composting every last one of these curses to Eden.

Swim

When the air on the roof is barbeque sweet
& a cigarette is slow
my life plays itself out into poems that fall
from themselves & then from my mouth as meteors
or bowls of butter love and seawater.

There is a breeze rustling my curtains
and it is prying a weight up unstuck to the floor
and stretching the cracks in the wood
into a gap that the goblins can crawl through.

All of this cackling haunting my head!
All of this *ACHE* in my chest
that translates to rage!

There are so many things that I am afraid to write about
because every word is a spell or a hex
and I need to cast the right magic
to fishhook my happy back.

I need to speak it into unbeing.
I need to sing it out of the song that is stuck in my head.

I need to show you my cave paintings.
I need to tell you about my hunger!

I need to show you my pricked fingers,
the creation needles I am using to stitch storybooks
out of scrapbook hindsight.
I need to scribble the letters, transfigure
this handful of alphabet into the wood blocks
that children piece together into triumphant towers and
telling their mothers, "look what I've made"

Mama,
Look what I've made!

Look at this handful of hot water burning my fingers!
See how the scalding is brewing the bittersweet coffee
steaming this room!

I need to show you the blisters.
I need to show you the scabs, how I picked at the sores
til the pot bubbled over.

I need to tell you that I did it by accident,
the night my mother found me on the kitchen floor
stuffed full of the boiling
& the hospital couldn't put my Humpty-Dumpty head
back together.

I tried to tell her that I did it by accident.
I tried to tell her that the atmosphere caught fire
& the thick smoke forced me to jump
like the snowflake bodies that floated down
from the twin towers
in a last ballet dance of bravery
leaping to a swift solution
because sometimes the only option is between
swift scalpel
& breakbone bludgeon.

Suicide is the kneejerk no one will ever suspect.
The rabid attack that will sneak up behind
from the depths of a stretch of placid ocean.

That snatching sea monster has been lurking
under the surface so long,
I've learned to count the anemone cells of its outline
& know not to venture out alone into the water

when the sun sinks down past my happy
or I'll be lost.

I don't want to be lost.
I don't want to watch my fingernails scraping the air
rushing up past my ears.
I don't want to domino any more bodies.

I don't want to die.

I need to write it.
I need to show you how I float.

This is my linguistic liferaft.
I am tapping tin tacks into a bad boat that might crumble
into the ashes of effort in low tide.
I am strapping lovers on as lifejackets.
I am unlatching my tragedies overboard
            as poetic deadweight.

I can either gag my gruesome truths up for a crowd,
                or drown.

On the good days, I'm swimming.

New Years on the Beach

The ocean wears the new year like a ballgown
she won't recycle. Her resolutions drift in and out.
Eternal promises don't keep the same timelines.
Linear ideas of 'success' are outdated, or ought to be.
This is the age of abstraction, divinity giving way
to profit and politics, capitalism's eternally upward arrows,
Earth's curves rewritten.
There are so many different ways to be on time.

In four seasons the landscape has shifted
four times. I sit in the same place and watch the tide
fill in gaps around me. I make resolutions
that sit in my gut and twist, build bridges
to cage myself on top of.

I think 'movement' is the same as 'freedom.'
        I want to live more fully,
I say, as though life were a paper cup
of gas station coffee.
How many ways are there to ask for more?

I write the year into the sand
& it is swallowed. Stars sing
behind a blanket of indifferent cloud. I swear they do.
Even joy can be a revolution.
There is no way to predict significance.
Even when there is no moon
the waves charge onwards with their armies of animals,
every moment a new year.

About the Author

Tyler Rose Mann is an internationally-based multidisciplinary artist.

Born in Brooklyn, NYC and raised in Mount Vernon, New York, she currently lives in Chiang Mai, Thailand and spends her time writing, painting, and volunteering with causes that promote environmental sustainability and human rights, with a focus on women's issues. She has discovered power and healing in art, and hopes that her words can be lifelines for the wounded and weapons for the disempowered.

Visit www.tylerrosemann.com to watch her live performances, explore her visual art and nonfiction writing, or book her for a commission or show.

72100625R00038

Made in the USA
Middletown, DE
03 May 2018